THE UNQUIET GRAVE
SHORT STORIES

The dead do not always lie quietly in their graves. Sometimes they have unfinished business with the living world, and want revenge for a wrong done to them. Perhaps in life they did wrong themselves and even in death can find no peace, so they must come back to bring trouble and fear to the living.

In these five stories the dead can come at any time, in any place, and in the strangest of ways – to an Oxford College, where Mr Williams is looking with interest at an old picture; or in bright sunshine to an inn where young Mr Thomson is spending his holiday. When the lights go out in Mr Edward Dunning's room and he reaches out to find the matches, what is it that his fingers touch in the dark? The wife and stepson of Squire Bowles have a question to ask, but only the Squire knows the answer, and how can you ask a question of a man who lies dead in his grave?

And when Professor Parkins blows an old whistle he has found, is it only the wind that answers, or something more? Something unseen, unheard, but more horrible than you could ever imagine . . .

OXFORD BOOKWORMS LIBRARY
Fantasy & Horror

The Unquiet Grave

SHORT STORIES

Stage 4 (1400 headwords)

Series Editor: Jennifer Bassett
Founder Editor: Tricia Hedge
Activities Editors: Jennifer Bassett and Alison Baxter

M. R. JAMES

The Unquiet Grave

SHORT STORIES

Retold by
Peter Hawkins

OXFORD UNIVERSITY PRESS

OXFORD
UNIVERSITY PRESS

Great Clarendon Street, Oxford OX2 6DP

Oxford University Press is a department of the University of Oxford
It furthers the University's objective of excellence in research, scholarship,
and education by publishing worldwide in

Oxford New York

Auckland Bangkok Buenos Aires Cape Town Chennai
Dar es Salaam Delhi Hong Kong Istanbul Karachi Kolkata
Kuala Lumpur Madrid Melbourne Mexico City Mumbai Nairobi
São Paulo Shanghai Singapore Taipei Tokyo Toronto

ISBN 0 19 423051 1

This simplified edition © Oxford University Press 2000

First published in Oxford Bookworms 1996
This second edition published in the Oxford Bookworms Library 2000
Fourth impression 2002

Illustrated by Paul Fisher Johnson

Typeset by Wyvern Typesetting Ltd, Bristol
Printed in Spain by Unigraf s.l.

CONTENTS

The Picture

For several years Mr Williams worked for the museum at the University of Oxford, enlarging its already famous collection of drawings and pictures of English country houses and churches. It is hard to imagine anything less alarming than collecting pictures of houses and churches, but Mr Williams found that even this peaceful work had its unexpected dark corners.

He bought many pictures for the museum from the London shop of Mr J. W. Britnell. Twice a year Mr Britnell sent a list of pictures to all his regular customers, who could then choose which pictures they wanted to look at before deciding whether to buy.

In February 1895 Mr Williams received a list from Mr Britnell with the following letter:

Dear Sir,
I think you might be interested in Picture Number 978 in our list, which I will be happy to send to you if you wish.
J. W. Britnell

Mr Williams turned to Number 978 in the list and found the following note:

Number 978. Artist unknown. Picture of an English

1

country house, early nineteenth century. 25 centimetres by 40 centimetres. £20.

It did not sound very interesting and the price seemed high. However, Mr Williams added it to the pictures that he asked Mr Britnell to send to him.

The pictures arrived at the museum one Saturday afternoon, just after Mr Williams had left. They were brought round to his rooms in college so that he could look at them over the weekend. Mr Williams found them on his table when he and his friend, Mr Binks, came in to have tea.

Picture Number 978 showed the front of quite a large country house. It had three rows of windows with the door in the middle of the bottom row. There were trees on both sides of the house and a large lawn in front of it. The letters A.W.F. were written in the corner of the picture. Mr Williams thought that it was not very well done, probably the work of an amateur artist, and he could not understand why Mr Britnell thought it was worth twenty pounds. He turned it over and saw that there was a piece of paper on the back with part of a name on it. All he could read were the ends of two lines of writing. The first said, '—ngly Hall'; the second, '—ssex'.

Mr Williams thought that it would be interesting to see if he could find the name of the house in one of his guidebooks before sending the picture back on Monday morning. Meanwhile, he put the picture on the table, lit the lamp because it was now getting dark, and made the tea.

While they were having tea, his friend picked up the picture, looked at it and said, 'Where's this house, Williams?'

'That's just what I was going to find out,' said Williams, taking a book from the shelf. 'If you look at the back, you'll see it's Something Hall in either Essex or Sussex. Half the name's missing, you see. I don't suppose you recognize the house, do you?'

'No, I don't,' said Mr Binks. 'It's from Britnell, I suppose, isn't it? Is it for the museum?'

'Well, I would buy it if the price was two pounds,' replied Mr Williams, 'but for some reason he wants twenty pounds for it. I can't think why. It's not a very good picture and there aren't even any figures in it to make it more interesting.'

'I agree it's not worth twenty pounds,' said Binks, 'but I don't think it's too bad. The light seems rather good to me and I think there is a figure here, just at the edge, in the front.'

'I think there is a figure here, just at the edge, in the front.'

3

'Let me see,' said Williams. 'Well, it's true the light is quite well done. Where's the figure? Oh, yes! Just the head, in the very front of the picture.'

And indeed there was – right on the edge of the picture – just the head of a man or a woman, who was looking towards the house. Williams had not noticed it before.

'Still,' he said, 'though it's better than I thought at first, I can't spend twenty pounds of the museum's money on a picture of a house I don't even know.'

Mr Binks, who had some work to finish, soon left and Mr Williams spent the time before dinner trying to find the name of the house in his guidebooks.

'If I knew the letter before the "—ngly",' he said to himself, 'it would be easy enough. But there are many more names ending in "—ngly" than I thought.'

Dinner in Mr Williams' college was at seven o'clock and afterwards a few of his friends came back to his rooms to play cards. During a pause in the game Mr Williams picked up the picture from the table without looking at it and passed it to a man named Garwood, who was interested in pictures. Garwood looked at it and said:

'This is really a very fine picture, you know, Williams. The light is very well done, in my opinion, and though the figure is rather unpleasant, it is quite interesting.'

'Yes, isn't it?' said Williams, who was too busy giving drinks to his guests to look at the picture again.

When his visitors had gone, Williams had to finish writing a letter, so it was after midnight before he was ready to go to

4

bed. The picture lay face upwards on the table where Garwood had left it and, as Williams was putting out the lamp, he saw it. For a moment he was too surprised to move, then he slowly picked up the picture and stared at it in horror. In the middle of the lawn, in front of the unknown house, there was a figure where there had been no figure earlier. It was crawling on hands and knees towards the house, and it was covered in a strange black garment with a white cross on the back.

After a second or two Mr Williams took the picture by one corner and carried it to an empty room. There, he locked it, face downwards, in a cupboard, then closed and locked the door of the empty room. He went back to his own room and locked the door behind him. Before going to bed, he sat down and wrote a note describing in detail the extraordinary change in the picture since he had received it.

He was glad to remember that Mr Garwood, who had looked at the picture earlier in the evening, had also seen a 'rather unpleasant' figure. He decided that in the morning he must ask someone to look carefully at the picture with him, and he must try very hard to discover the name of the house. He would ask his neighbour, Mr Nisbet, to have breakfast with him. Then he would spend the morning looking for the house in his guidebooks.

Mr Nisbet arrived at nine o'clock and the two men sat down to breakfast. When they had finished, Mr Williams, feeling both nervous and excited, hurried to the empty room. He unlocked the cupboard, took out the picture, still face

5

downwards, and, without looking at it, went back to his own room and put it into Nisbet's hands.

'Now, Nisbet,' he said, 'I want you to tell me what you see in that picture. Describe it, please, in detail. I'll tell you why afterwards.'

'Well,' said Nisbet, 'I have here a picture of an English country house by moonlight.'

'Moonlight? Are you sure?'

'Oh, yes. The moon is shown quite clearly and there are clouds in the sky.'

'All right. Go on. But I'm sure,' added Williams quietly, 'that there was no moon when I first saw it.'

'Well, there's not much more I can say,' Nisbet continued. 'The house has three rows of windows, five in each row, except at the bottom, where there's a door instead of the middle one and . . .'

'But what about figures?' said Williams with great interest.

'Figures?' replied Nisbet. 'There aren't any.'

'What? No figure on the grass in front?'

'No. Not a thing.'

'Are you sure?'

'Of course I am. But there's one other thing.'

'What's that?'

'One of the windows on the ground floor, on the left of the door, is open.'

'Is it really? Oh dear! I suppose he's got into the house,' said Williams, with great excitement.

He hurried across to where Nisbet was sitting and, taking

the picture from him, saw for himself. It was quite true. There was no figure on the lawn, and there was the open window.

For a moment Williams was too surprised to speak, then he sat down at his desk and wrote for a few minutes. When

It was quite true. There was no figure on the lawn,
and there was the open window.

he had finished, he brought two papers across to Nisbet. He asked him to sign the first one, which was Nisbet's own description of the picture, then to read the other one, which was the note Williams had written the night before.

'What can it all mean?' asked Nisbet.

'That's what I must find out,' said Williams. 'Now, there are three things I must do. First, I must ask Garwood exactly what he saw when he looked at the picture last night, then I must have the picture photographed before it goes any further and, thirdly, I must find out where this house is.'

'I can take the photograph for you myself,' said Nisbet. 'But, you know, I think we are seeing something terrible happening here. The question is, has it already happened or is it going to happen? You really must find out where this house is.' He looked at the picture again and shook his head. 'I think you are right, you know. He *has* got in. I'm sure there will be some trouble in that house.'

'I'll tell you what I'll do,' said Williams. 'I'll show the picture to old Doctor Green. He grew up in Essex and he often goes to Sussex to see his brother who lives there. He's been going there for years. He must know both places quite well.'

'That's a very good idea,' agreed Nisbet. 'But I think I heard Green say that he was going away this weekend.'

'You're right,' said Williams. 'I remember now – he's gone to Brighton for the weekend. I'll leave a note asking him to see me as soon as he returns. Meanwhile, you take the picture and photograph it and I'll see Garwood and ask him what he saw when he looked at it last night.' He paused. 'You know,' he added, 'I don't think twenty pounds is too much to ask for this picture, after all.'

In a short time Williams returned to his room, bringing Mr Garwood with him. Mr Garwood said that when he had looked at the picture the figure was just starting to crawl across the lawn. He remembered that it was wearing a black garment with something white on the back – he was not sure if it was a cross. While he was writing this down, Mr Nisbet returned and said that he had photographed the picture.

'What are you going to do now, Williams?' asked Mr Garwood. 'Are you going to sit and watch the picture all day?'

'No, I don't think we need to do that,' replied Williams. 'You see, there has been plenty of time since I looked at it last night for the creature in the picture to finish what he wants to do, but he has only gone into the house. The window is open and he must still be in there. I think he wants us to see what happens next. Anyway, I don't think the picture will change much during the day. I suggest that we all go for a walk after lunch and come back here for tea. I'll leave the picture on my table and lock the door. My servant has a key and can get in if he wants to, but nobody else can.'

The others agreed that this was a good plan. They also wanted to avoid talking to anyone about this extraordinary picture, knowing what excitement and argument it would cause.

At about five o'clock they came back to Mr Williams' rooms for tea. When they entered the room, they were surprised to find Mr Filcher, the servant, sitting in Mr Williams' armchair and staring in horror at the picture on the table. Mr Filcher had worked in the college for many years and had never before behaved in so unusual a way. He seemed to feel this himself, and tried to jump to his feet when the three men came in.

'I'm sorry, sir,' he said. 'I didn't mean to sit down.'

'That's all right, Robert,' said Mr Williams. 'I was going to ask you some time what you thought of that picture.'

'Well, sir,' replied the servant, 'of course, I don't really understand pictures, but I wouldn't like my little girl to see it. I'm sure it would give her bad dreams. It doesn't seem the right kind of picture to leave lying around. It could frighten anybody – seeing that awful thing carrying off the poor baby. That's what I think, sir. Will you need me any more today, sir? Thank you, sir.'

Filcher left the room and the three men went at once to look at the picture. There was the house as before, under the moon and the clouds. But the window that had been open was now shut, and the figure was once more on the lawn; but not crawling this time. Now it was walking, with long steps, towards the front of the picture. The moon was behind it and the black material of its garment nearly covered its face. The three men were deeply thankful that they could see no more of the face than a high, white forehead and a few long, thin hairs. Its legs beneath the garment were horribly thin, and its arms held something which seemed to be a child, whether dead or living it was not possible to say.

10

The three friends watched the picture until it was time for dinner but it did not change at all. They hurried back to Williams' rooms as soon as dinner was finished. The picture was where they had left it, but the figure had gone, and the house was quiet under the moon and the clouds.

Its arms held something which seemed to be a child.

11

'Well,' said Mr Williams, 'now we really must try to find where this house is.' They got out the guidebooks and began to work.

It was nearly two hours later when Williams suddenly cried, 'Ha! This looks like it!'

He read aloud from the *Guide to Essex* that he was holding:

'Anningly. Interesting twelfth-century church containing the tombs of the Francis family, whose home, Anningly Hall, stands just behind the church. The family is now extinct. The last member of the family disappeared very mysteriously in 1802 while still a child. His father, Sir Arthur Francis, a well-known amateur artist, lived quite alone after that until he was found dead in his house three years later, after he had just completed a picture of the Hall.'

As Mr Williams finished reading, there was a knock on the door and Doctor Green came in. He had just returned from Brighton and had found Williams' note. He agreed at once that the picture was of Anningly Hall, which was not far from where he had grown up.

'Have you any explanation of the figure, Green?' asked Williams.

'I don't know, I'm sure, Williams,' Doctor Green replied. 'When I was a boy, some of the old people in Anningly still used to talk about the disappearance of the Francis child. They said that Sir Arthur had a lot of trouble with some of the local people coming onto his land to steal his fish and his birds. He decided to catch them all and have them punished, and, one by one he did, until there was only one left. This was a man called Gawdy whose family had once been rich and important in that part of Essex. In fact, some of them had their tombs in the village church too. However, the family had lost all their land and their money over the years and Gawdy felt rather bitter about it all. For a long time Sir Arthur could not catch him doing anything wrong until one night his men found Gawdy with some dead birds in Sir Arthur's woods. There was a fight and one of the men was shot. This was just what Sir Arthur needed; the judge was all on his side, of course, and poor Gawdy was hanged a few days later. People thought that some friend of Gawdy's stole Sir Arthur's little boy in revenge, to put an end to the Francis family as well. But I should say now, that it looks more as if old Gawdy managed the job himself. Brrrr. I don't like to think about it. Let's have a drink, shall we?'

The story of the picture was told to a few people; some believed it and some did not. Mr Britnell knew nothing about it except that the picture was unusual in some way. It is now in the museum and, although it has been carefully watched, no one has ever seen it change again.

Rats

'And if you walked through the bedrooms now, you'd see the dirty grey bedsheets rising and falling like the waves of the sea.'

'Rising and falling with what?'

'Why, with the rats crawling underneath them.'

But was it rats? I ask, because in another story it was not. I cannot put a date to the story, but I was young when I heard it, and the teller was old.

It happened in Suffolk, at a place where the coast road climbs a little hill as it travels northwards. At the top of the hill, on the left, stands a tall narrow house built about 1770. Behind it are the gardens and other buildings, and in front lies open heath with a view of the distant sea. The house was once a well-known inn, though I believe few people stay there now.

To this inn came Mr Thomson, a young man from the University of Cambridge, in search of peace and pleasant surroundings in which to study. He found both; the innkeeper and his wife kept a comfortable house, and Mr Thomson was the only guest.

It was fine spring weather and Mr Thomson's days passed

very happily. His plan was to stay a month: studying all morning, walking on the heath in the afternoon, and talking with the local people in the bar in the evening.

On one of his walks over the heath he came upon a large white stone with a square hole in the top. No doubt it had once held a post of some kind. He looked around him at the wide, open heath and beyond that, the sea shining in the bright sunlight and decided that the stone had probably once held a sign to guide the local sailors back to their homes.

In the bar that evening he spoke of the stone and his idea that it had, perhaps, once held a sign to guide sailors.

'Yes,' said Mr Betts, the innkeeper, 'I've heard they could see it from out at sea, but whatever was there fell down long before our time.'

'A good thing it did, too,' said one of the villagers. 'It wasn't a lucky sign – that's what the old men used to say. Not lucky for the fishing, I mean.'

'Why ever not?' said Thomson.

'Well, I never saw it myself,' answered the other. 'But those old fishermen had some strange ideas, and I wouldn't be surprised if they pulled it down themselves.'

It was impossible to get anything clearer than this, and people soon began to talk about something else.

One day Mr Thomson decided not to have a walk in the afternoon, but to continue studying. He returned to his room after an early lunch and read on until about three o'clock. Then he put down his book, rose and went out into the passage, thinking that he would have a rest for five minutes.

The house was completely silent. He remembered that it was market day and everyone had gone into the local town.

As he stood there, the idea came to him to look at the four other rooms along the passage. He was sure that the Bettses would not mind. The room opposite his was big but had no view of the sea. The next two were both smaller than his with only one window each – his had two. He walked down the passage to the door at the end and found that it was locked. Thomson decided that he must see inside that room; perhaps the key of his room would unlock the door. It did not, so he fetched the keys from the other three rooms and tried them. One of them fitted the lock and he opened the door.

The room had two windows looking south and west, and hot bright sunshine filled the room. Here there was no carpet, only wooden floorboards; no pictures, no furniture, except a bed in the farther corner – a metal bed covered with a bluish-grey blanket. You could not imagine a more ordinary room, but there was something that made Thomson close the door very quickly and very quietly behind him, and then lean against the wall in the passage, trembling all over.

Under the blanket someone lay, and not only lay, but moved. It was certainly some *one* and not some *thing*, because the shape of the head and body was clear under the blanket. However, it was all covered, and no one lies with covered head except a dead person; and this was not dead, not truly dead, because it was moving and shaking.

Thomson tried to tell himself that he was imagining things, but on this bright sunny day that was impossible. What should

he do? First, lock the door again. With a trembling hand he
turned the key in the lock, but as he did so, it made a little
noise, and at once soft footsteps were heard coming towards
the door. Thomson ran to his room and locked himself in,
although he knew it was useless. How could doors and locks
stop what he suspected? He stood listening for several
minutes, but no sound came from the passage.

With a trembling hand he turned the key in the lock.

Now he could not think what to do. He wanted to pack
his bags and leave the inn at once, but only that morning he
had told Mr and Mrs Betts that he would stay for another
week. If he left suddenly, they would surely guess the reason.

Then he thought, either the Bettses knew about the creature in that room but still stayed in the house, or they knew nothing about it. Perhaps they knew just enough to make them keep the room locked, but not enough to make them leave the house. In any case, they did not seem to be afraid of whatever was in that room, so why should he be afraid of it? He decided to stay another week as he had arranged.

As the days passed, Thomson listened hard for sounds from the room at the end of the passage, but he heard nothing. Of course he could not ask Mr or Mrs Betts about it, and he did not think he could ask anyone else. However, he wanted very much to find some kind of explanation, so he decided that he would try to see inside the locked room once again before he left the inn.

He made a simple plan. He would arrange to leave by an afternoon train and would have his luggage put on the cart for the station. Then, just before leaving, he would go back upstairs to make sure that he had not left anything behind. But, instead of going to his own room, he would go to the other. He put oil on the key to make it easier to open the door quietly.

His last day arrived. After lunch his luggage was taken downstairs and put on the cart for the station. Mr and Mrs Betts came to the front door to say goodbye. Thomson thanked them for making him so comfortable and they thanked him for staying with them. Then, as he had planned, Thomson said:

'I'll just check that I haven't left a book or anything in my room. No, please don't worry, I can do it myself.'

He hurried up the stairs to the locked room, turned the key quietly and opened the door. He almost laughed aloud. Leaning, or perhaps sitting, on the edge of the bed was – nothing more than an ordinary scarecrow! A scarecrow out of the garden, of course, just put away in the empty room . . .

Yes; but suddenly amusement stopped. Do scarecrows have bony feet? Do their heads roll from side to side on their shoulders? Have they got heavy metal chains around their necks? Can they get up and move across the floor, with rolling head and arms close at their sides . . . and shake with the cold?

Thomson shut the door with a bang, jumped down the stairs and fell in a faint at the door of the inn. When he became conscious again, Mr Betts was standing over him with a glass of whisky and a serious face.

'You shouldn't do it, sir,' said Betts. 'You shouldn't go looking into people's secrets, especially when they've done their best to make you comfortable.'

Thomson said that he was very sorry but the innkeeper and his wife found it hard to accept his apologies.

'Who knows what damage it will do to the good name of the inn?' said Mr Betts, and his wife agreed.

At last Thomson managed to make Mr and Mrs Betts believe that he would not say anything about what he had seen. By that time he had missed his train but he decided to go into town and spend the night at the Station Hotel.

Before he went, Mr Betts told him what little he knew.

'They say he used to be the innkeeper here many years ago, and he worked with the thieves who robbed and murdered travellers on the heath. That's why he was hanged – in chains, they say, up at the gallows on that white stone you saw. Yes, the fishermen pulled the gallows down, I

'*That's why he was hanged – in chains, they say.*'

believe, because they saw it out at sea, and they said it kept the fish away. We heard all this from the people who sold us the inn. "You keep that room shut up," they said, "but don't move the bed out, and you'll find there won't be any trouble." And we haven't had any trouble. He hasn't once come out into the house, though who knows what he might do now? I've never seen him myself, and I don't want to. But I do hope you'll keep it a secret, sir. If word gets out, people won't want to come and stay here, will they?'

The promise of silence was kept for many years. I heard the story when Mr Thomson, now an old man, came to stay with my father. I was told to take him up to his room, but when we got there, Mr Thomson stepped forward and threw the door open himself. He stood there in the doorway for some moments, looking carefully into every corner of the room.

Then he turned to me. 'I beg your pardon,' he said. 'A strange way to behave, I know. But there is a very good reason for it.'

A few days later I heard what the reason was, and you have heard it now.

Casting the Runes

15th April 1902

Dear Mr Karswell

I am returning your paper on 'The Truth of Alchemy', which you have kindly offered to read at our next club meeting. Unfortunately, we do not feel able to accept your offer.

W. Gayton, Secretary

18th April 1902

Dear Mr Karswell

I am afraid that I am not able to arrange a meeting with you to discuss your offer to read a paper on alchemy. However, the club considered your offer most carefully, and we did not refuse it until we had asked for the opinion of an expert in these matters.

W. Gayton, Secretary

20th April 1902

The Secretary writes to inform Mr Karswell that it is impossible for him to give the name of any person or persons who were asked for an opinion on Mr Karswell's paper on alchemy. The Secretary also wishes to say that he cannot reply to any further letters on this matter.

'And who *is* Mr Karswell?' asked the Secretary's wife.

She had called at his office and had just picked up and read the last of these letters.

'Well, my dear,' replied her husband, 'just at present Mr Karswell is a very angry man. All I know about him is that he's rich, lives at Lufford Abbey in Warwickshire, and considers himself to be an alchemist. And I don't want to meet him for the next week or two. Now, shall we go?'

'What have you been doing to make him angry?' asked the Secretary's wife.

'The usual thing, my dear. He sent us a paper which he wanted to read at our next meeting. We showed it to Edward Dunning – almost the only man in England who knows about these things – and he said it was no good, so we refused it. Now Karswell wants to see me about it and to find out whose opinion we asked for. Well, you've seen my reply to that. Of course, you mustn't say anything about it to anyone.'

'You know very well that I would never do a thing like that. Indeed, I hope he doesn't discover that it was poor Mr Dunning.'

'Why do you say "poor" Mr Dunning?' said the Secretary. 'He's a very happy man and quite rich, I believe. He has a comfortable home and plenty of time to spend on his hobbies.'

'I only meant that I would be sorry for him if Mr Karswell discovered his name and made trouble for him.'

'Oh yes! He would be poor Mr Dunning then,' agreed her husband.

* * *

The Secretary and his wife were lunching with friends that day, a Mr and Mrs Bennett, who came from Warwickshire. Mrs Gayton decided to ask them if they knew Mr Karswell. However, before she could do so, Mrs Bennett said to her husband:

'I saw Mr Karswell this morning. He was coming out of the British Museum as I was driving past.'

'Did you really?' said her husband. 'I wonder what brings him up to London.'

'Is he a friend of yours?' asked the Secretary, smiling at his wife.

'Oh no!' said Mr and Mrs Bennett together.

'He's one of our neighbours in Warwickshire,' explained Mrs Bennett, 'but he's not at all popular. Nobody knows what he does with his time and they say he believes in all kinds of strange and unpleasant things. If he thinks you have been impolite to him, he never forgets it, and he never does anything kind for his neighbours.'

'But, my dear,' said her husband, 'you're forgetting the Christmas party he gave for the children.'

'Oh no, I'm not,' replied his wife. 'That's a good example of what I mean.' She turned to the Secretary and his wife. 'The first winter he was at Lufford this horrible man invited all the village children to a Christmas party at his house. He said that he had some of these new moving pictures to show them. Everyone was rather surprised because they thought that he didn't like children; he used to be very angry if any of the village children came on to his land. However, the children

24

all went and a friend of ours, Mr Farrer, went with them to see that everything was all right.'

'And was it?' asked the Secretary.

'Indeed it was not!' replied Mrs Bennett. 'Our friend said it was obvious that Mr Karswell wanted to frighten the children to death, and he very nearly did so. The first film was "Red Riding Hood", and the wolf was so terrible that several of the smaller children had to leave the room. The other films were more and more frightening. At the end Mr Karswell showed a film of a little boy in the park surrounding Lufford Abbey – every child in the room could recognize the place. There was a horrible creature in white following the little boy. At first you could see it hiding in the trees, then it became clearer and clearer and at last it caught the little boy and pulled him to pieces. Our friend said that it gave him some very bad dreams, so you can imagine how the children felt. Of course, this was too much and Mr Farrer told Karswell that he must stop it. All Mr Karswell said was: "Oh! The dear children want to go home to bed, do they? Very well, just one last picture."

'And then he showed a short film of horrible creatures with wings and lots of legs. They seemed to be crawling out of the picture to get among the children. Of course, the children were terribly frightened and they all started screaming and running out of the room. Some of them were quite badly hurt because they were all trying to get out of the room at the same time. There was the most awful trouble in the village afterwards. Several of the fathers wanted to go to Lufford

Abbey and break all the windows, but the gates were locked when they got there. So you see why Mr Karswell is not one of our friends.'

'Yes,' agreed her husband. 'I think Karswell is a very dangerous man. I feel sorry for anyone who makes an enemy of him.'

'Is he the man,' asked the Secretary, 'who wrote a *History of Witchcraft* about ten years ago?'

'Yes, that's the man,' replied Mr Bennett. 'Do you remember what the newspapers said about it?'

'Yes, I do,' said the Secretary. 'They all said that it was a really bad book. In fact, I knew the man who wrote the sharpest report of them all. So did you, of course. You remember John Harrington? He was at Cambridge with us.'

'Oh, very well indeed. But I had heard nothing of him between the time we left university and the day I read about his accident in the newspaper.'

'What happened to him?' asked one of the ladies.

'It was very strange,' said Mr Bennett. 'He fell out of a tree and broke his neck. The mystery was why he had climbed the tree in the first place. There he was, an ordinary man walking home along a country road late one evening, and suddenly he began to run as fast as he could. Finally he climbed up a tree beside the road; a dead branch broke, he fell and was killed. When they found him the next morning, he had a terrible expression of fear on his face. It was quite clear that he had been chased by something and people talked about mad dogs and so on, but no one ever found the answer.

Suddenly he began to run as fast as he could.

That was in 1889 and ever since then his brother, Henry, who was also at Cambridge with us, has been trying to find out the truth of what happened. He thinks that someone wanted to harm his brother but, of course, he has never been able to prove anything.'

After a pause Mr Bennett asked the Secretary, 'Did you ever read Karswell's *History of Witchcraft*?'

'Yes, I did,' said the Secretary.

'And was it as bad as Harrington said?'

'Oh yes. It was badly written but what it said was very

27

bad too, although Karswell seemed to believe every word of what he was saying.'

'I didn't read the book but I remember what Harrington wrote about it,' said Mr Bennett. 'If anyone wrote like that about one of my books, I would never write another, I'm sure.'

'I don't think Karswell feels the same way,' replied the Secretary. 'But it's half past three; we must go. Thank you for an excellent lunch.'

On the way home Mrs Gayton said, 'I hope that horrible man Karswell doesn't discover that it was Mr Dunning who said his paper was no good.'

'I don't think he's likely to do that,' replied her husband. 'Dunning won't tell him and neither shall I. The only way Karswell might find out is by asking the people at the British Museum Library for the name of anyone who studies all their old books about alchemy. Let's hope he won't think of that.'

But Mr Karswell was a very clever man.

One evening, later in the same week, Mr Edward Dunning was returning from the British Museum Library, where he had been working all day, to his comfortable home. He lived alone there, except for the two women who cooked and cleaned for him. A train took him most of the way home, then he caught a bus for the last mile or two. He had finished reading his newspaper by the time he got on the bus so he amused himself by reading the different notices on the windows opposite him. He already knew most of them quite well, but there seemed to be a new one in the corner that he had not seen before. It was yellow with blue letters, and all he could read was the name 'John Harrington'. Soon the bus was nearly empty and he changed his seat so that he could read the rest of it. It said:

REMEMBER JOHN HARRINGTON OF THE LAURELS, ASHBROOKE, WARWICKSHIRE, WHO DIED 18TH SEPTEMBER 1889. HE WAS ALLOWED THREE MONTHS.

Mr Dunning stared at this notice for a long time. He was the only passenger on the bus when it reached his stop, and as he was getting off, he said to the driver, 'I was looking at that new notice on the window, the blue and yellow one. It's rather strange, isn't it?'

'Which one is that, sir?' asked the driver. 'I don't think I know it.'

'Why, this one here,' said Mr Dunning, turning to point to it. Then he suddenly stopped – the window was now quite clear. The blue and yellow notice, with its strange message, had completely disappeared.

'But I'm sure . . .' Mr Dunning began, staring at the window. Then he turned back to the driver. 'I'm sorry. Perhaps I imagined it,' he said.

He hurried off the bus and walked home, feeling rather worried. The notice *had* been there on the window; he was sure of it. But what possible explanation could there be for its disappearing like that?

The following afternoon Mr Dunning was walking from the British Museum to the station when he saw, some way ahead of him, a man holding some leaflets, ready to give to people as they passed. However, Mr Dunning did not see him give anyone a leaflet until he himself reached the place. One was pushed into his hand as he passed. The man's hand touched his, and gave Mr Dunning an unpleasant surprise. The hand seemed unnaturally rough and hot. As Mr Dunning walked on, he looked quickly at the leaflet and noticed the name Harrington. He stopped in alarm, and felt in his pocket for his glasses, but in that second someone took the leaflet out of his hand. He turned quickly – but whoever it was had disappeared, and so had the man with the leaflets.

The next day in the British Museum he was arranging his papers on the desk when he thought he heard his own name whispered behind him. He turned round hurriedly, knocking some of his papers on to the floor, but saw no one he recognized. He picked up his papers and was beginning to work when a large man at the table behind him, who was just getting up to leave, touched him on the shoulder.

'May I give you these?' he said, holding out a number of papers. 'I think they must be yours.'

'Yes, they are mine. Thank you,' said Mr Dunning. A moment later the man had left the room.

Later, Mr Dunning asked the librarian if he knew the large man's name.

'Oh yes. That's Mr Karswell,' said the librarian. 'In fact, he asked me the other day who were the experts on alchemy, so I told him that you were the only one in the country. I'll introduce you if you like; I'm sure he'd like to meet you.'

'No, no, please don't,' said Dunning. 'He is someone I would very much prefer to avoid.'

On the way home from the museum Mr Dunning felt strangely unwell. Usually he looked forward to an evening spent alone with his books, but now he wanted to be with other people. Unfortunately, the train and the bus were unusually empty. When he reached his house, he was surprised to find the doctor waiting for him.

'I'm sorry, Dunning,' said the doctor. 'I'm afraid I've had to send both your servants to hospital.'

'Oh dear!' said Mr Dunning. 'What's the matter with them?'

'They told me they'd bought some fish for their lunch from a man who came to the door, and it has made them quite ill.'

'I'm very sorry to hear that,' said Mr Dunning.

'It's strange,' said the doctor. 'I've spoken to the neighbours and no one else has seen anyone selling fish. Now, don't worry. They're not seriously ill, but I'm afraid they won't be home for two or three days. Why don't you come and have dinner with me this evening? Eight o'clock. You know where I live.'

Mr Dunning enjoyed his evening with the doctor and returned to his lonely house at half past eleven. He had got into bed and was almost asleep when he heard quite clearly the sound of his study door opening downstairs. Alarmed, he got out of bed, went to the top of the stairs, and listened. There were no sounds of movements or footsteps, but he suddenly felt warm, even hot, air round his legs. He went

31

He went to the top of the stairs, and listened.

back and decided to lock himself into his room, and then
suddenly, the electric lights all went out. He put out his hand
to find the matches on the table beside the bed – and touched
a mouth, with teeth and with hair around it, and not, he said

later, the mouth of a human being. In less than a second he was in another room and had locked the door. And there he spent a miserable night, in the dark, expecting every moment to hear something trying to open the door. But nothing came.

When it grew light, he went nervously back into his bedroom and searched it. Everything was in its usual place. He searched the whole house, but found nothing.

It was a miserable day for Mr Dunning. He did not want to go to the British Museum in case he met Karswell, and he did not feel comfortable in the empty house. He spent half an hour at the hospital where he found that the two women were feeling much better. Then he decided to go to the Club for lunch. There, he was very glad to find his friend the Secretary and they had lunch together. He told Gayton that his servants were in hospital, but he was unwilling to speak of his other problems.

'You poor man,' said the Secretary. 'We can't leave you alone with no one to cook your meals. You must come and stay with us. My wife and I will be delighted to have you. Go home after lunch and bring your things to my house this afternoon. No, I won't let you refuse.'

In fact, Mr Dunning was very happy to accept his friend's invitation. The idea of spending another night alone in his house was alarming him more and more.

At dinner that evening Mr Dunning looked so unwell that the Gaytons felt sorry for him and tried to make him forget his troubles. But later, when the two men were alone, Dunning became very quiet again. Suddenly he said:

'Gayton, I think that man Karswell knows that I was the person who advised you to refuse his paper.'

Gayton looked surprised. 'What makes you think that?' he asked.

So Dunning explained. 'I don't really mind,' he continued, 'but I believe that he's not a very nice person and it could be difficult if we met.'

After this Dunning sat in silence, looking more and more miserable. At last Gayton asked him if some serious trouble was worrying him.

'Oh! I'm so glad you asked,' said Dunning. 'I feel I really must talk to someone about it. Do you know anything about a man named John Harrington?'

Very surprised, Gayton could only ask why he wanted to know. Then Dunning told him the whole story of the notice in the bus, the man with the leaflets, and what had happened in his own house. He ended by asking again if Gayton knew anything about John Harrington.

Now it was the Secretary who was worried and did not quite know how to answer. His friend was clearly in a very nervous condition, and the story of Harrington's death was alarming for anyone to hear. Was it possible that Karswell was involved with both men? In the end Gayton said only that he had known Harrington at Cambridge and believed that he had died suddenly in 1889. He added a few details about the man and his books.

Later, when they were alone, the Secretary discussed the matter with his wife. Mrs Gayton said immediately that

Karswell must be the link between the two men, and she wondered if Harrington's brother, Henry, could perhaps help Mr Dunning. She would ask the Bennetts where Henry Harrington lived, and then bring the two men together.

When they met, the first thing Dunning told Henry Harrington was of the strange ways in which he had learnt his brother's name. He described his other recent experiences and asked Harrington what he remembered about his brother before he died.

'John was in a very strange condition for some time before his death, it's true,' replied Henry Harrington. 'Among other things, he felt that someone was following him all the time. I'm sure that someone was trying to harm him, and your story reminds me very much of the things he experienced. Could there be any link between you and my brother, do you think?'

'Well,' replied Dunning, 'there is just one thing. I'm told that your brother wrote some very hard things about a book not long before he died and, as it happens, I too have done something to annoy the man who wrote that book.'

'Don't tell me his name is Karswell,' said Harrington.

'Why yes, it is,' replied Dunning.

Henry Harrington looked very serious.

'Well, that is the final proof I needed,' he said. 'Let me explain. I believe that my brother John was sure that this man Karswell was trying to harm him. Now, John was very fond of music. He often went to concerts in London, and always kept the concert programmes afterwards. About three

35

months before he died, he came back from a concert and showed me the programme.

'"I nearly missed this one," he said. "I couldn't find mine at the end of the concert and was looking everywhere for it. Then my neighbour offered me his, saying that he didn't need it any more. I don't know who he was – he was a very large man."

'Soon after this my brother told me that he felt very uncomfortable at night. Then, one evening, he was looking through all his concert programmes when he found something strange in the programme that his large neighbour had given him. It was a thin piece of paper with some writing on it – not normal writing. It looked to me more like Runic letters in red and black. Well, we were looking at this and wondering how to give it back to its owner when the door opened and the wind blew the paper into the fire. It was burnt in a moment.'

Mr Dunning sat silent as Harrington paused.

'Now,' he continued, 'I don't know if you ever read that book of Karswell's, *The History of Witchcraft,* which my brother said was so badly written.'

Dunning shook his head.

'Well,' Harrington went on, 'after my brother died I read some of it. The book was indeed badly written and a lot of it was rubbish, but one bit caught my eye. It was about "Casting the Runes" on people in order to harm them, and I'm sure that Karswell was writing from personal experience. I won't tell you all the details, but I'm certain that the large man at the concert was Karswell, and that the paper he gave my brother caused his death. Now, I must ask you if anything similar has happened to you.'

Dunning told him what had happened in the British Museum.

'So Karswell did actually pass you some papers?' said Harrington. 'Have you checked them? No? Well, I think we should do so at once, if you agree.'

They went round to Dunning's empty house where his papers were lying on the table. As he picked them up, a thin piece of paper fell to the ground. A sudden wind blew it towards the open window, but Harrington closed the window just in time to stop the paper escaping. He caught the paper in his hand.

'I thought so,' he said. 'It looks just like the one my brother was given. I think you're in great danger, Dunning.'

The two men discussed the problem for a long time. The paper was covered in Runic letters which they could not understand, but both men felt certain that the message, whatever it was, could bring unknown horrors to its owner. They agreed that the paper must be returned to Karswell, and that the only safe and sure way was to give it to him in person and see that he accepted it. This would be difficult since Karswell knew what Dunning looked like.

'I can grow a beard,' said Dunning, 'so that he won't recognize me. But who knows when the end will come?'

'I think I know,' said Harrington. 'The concert where my brother was given the paper was on June 18th, and he died on September 18th, three months later.'

'Perhaps it will be the same for me,' Dunning said miserably. He looked in his diary. 'Yes, April 23rd was the day in the Museum – that brings me to July 23rd. Now, Harrington, I would very much like to know anything you can tell me about your brother's trouble.'

'The thing that worried him most,' said Harrington, 'was the feeling that whenever he was alone, someone was watching him. After a time I began to sleep in his room, and he felt better because of that. But he talked a lot in his sleep.'

The paper was covered in runic letters.

'What about?' asked Dunning.

'I think it would be better not to go into details about that,' replied Harrington. 'But I remember that he received a packet by post, which contained a little diary. My brother didn't look at it, but after his death I did, and found that all the pages after September 18th had been cut out. Perhaps you wonder why he went out alone on the evening he died? The strange thing is that during the last week of his life all his worries seemed to disappear, and he no longer felt that someone was watching or following him.'

Finally, the two men made a plan. Harrington had a friend who lived near Lufford Abbey; he would stay with him and watch Karswell. If he thought they had a chance to arrange an accidental meeting, he would send a telegram to Dunning. Meanwhile, Dunning had to be ready to move at any moment and had to keep the paper safe.

Harrington went off to his friend in Warwickshire and Dunning was left alone. He found waiting very hard, and was unable to work or to take any interest in anything. He felt that he was living in a black cloud that cut him off from the world. He became more and more worried as May, June, and the first half of July passed with no word from Harrington. But all this time Karswell remained at Lufford Abbey.

At last, less than a week before July 23rd, Dunning received a telegram from his friend:

Karswell is leaving London for France on the boat train on Thursday night. Be ready. I will come to you tonight. Harrington.

When he arrived, the two men made their final plan. The boat train from London stopped only once before Dover, at Croydon West. Harrington would get on the train in London and find where Karswell was sitting. Dunning would wait for the train at Croydon West where Harrington would look out for him. Dunning would make sure that his name was not on his luggage and, most importantly, must have the paper with him.

On Thursday night Dunning waited impatiently for the train at Croydon West. He now had a thick beard and was wearing glasses, and felt sure that Karswell would not recognize him. He noticed that he no longer felt himself to be in danger, but this only made him worry more, because he remembered what Harrington had said about his brother's last week.

At last the boat train arrived and he saw his friend at one of the windows. It was important not to show that they knew each other, so Dunning got on further down the train and slowly made his way to the right compartment.

Harrington and Karswell were alone in the compartment, and Dunning entered and sat in the corner furthest from Karswell. Karswell's heavy travelling coat and bag were on the seat opposite him, and next to where Dunning was now sitting. Dunning thought of hiding the paper in the coat but realized that this would not do; he would have to give it to Karswell and see that Karswell accepted it. Could he hide Karswell's bag in some way, put the paper in it, and then give the bag to him as he got off the train? This was the only plan he could think of. He wished desperately that he could ask Harrington's advice.

Karswell himself seemed very restless. Twice he stood up to look out of the window. Dunning was just going to try to make his bag fall off the seat when he saw a warning expression in Harrington's eye – Karswell was watching them in the window.

Then Karswell stood up a third time, opened the window and put his head outside. As he stood up, something fell silently to the floor and Dunning saw that it was a thin wallet containing Karswell's tickets. In a moment Dunning had pushed the paper into the pocket at the back of the wallet. Just then the train began to lose speed as it came into Dover station, and Karswell closed the window and turned round.

'May I give you this, sir? I think it must be yours,' said Dunning, holding out the wallet.

'Oh, thank you, sir,' replied Karswell, checking that they were his tickets. Then he put the wallet into his pocket.

Suddenly the compartment seemed to grow dark and very hot, but already Harrington and Dunning were opening the door and getting off the train.

Dunning, unable to stand up, sat on a seat on the platform breathing deeply, while Harrington followed Karswell the little way to the boat. He saw Karswell show his ticket to the ticket collector and pass on to the boat. As he did so, the official called after him:

'Excuse me, sir. Has your friend got a ticket?'

'What d'you mean, my friend?' shouted Karswell angrily.

'Sorry, sir. I thought there was someone with you,' apologized the ticket collector. He turned to another official beside him, 'Did he have a dog with him or something? I was sure there were two of them.'

Five minutes later there was nothing except the disappearing lights of the boat, the night wind, and the moon.

'May I give you this, sir? I think it must be yours.'

That night the two friends sat up late in their room in the hotel. Although the danger was past, a worry remained.

'Harrington,' Dunning said, 'I'm afraid we have sent a man to his death.'

'He murdered my brother,' replied Harrington, 'and he tried to murder you. It is right that he should die.'

'Don't you think we should warn him?' asked Dunning.

'How can we?' replied his friend. 'We don't know where he's going.'

'He's going to Abbeville,' said Dunning. 'I saw it on his ticket. Today is the 21st. We could send a telegram in the morning to all the main hotels in Abbeville saying: *Check your ticket wallet. Dunning.* Then he would have a whole day.'

After a pause Harrington agreed. 'I see it would make you feel happier,' he said, 'so we'll warn him.'

The telegrams were sent first thing in the morning but no one knows if Karswell received any of them. All that is known is that on July 23rd a man was looking at the front of a church in Abbeville when a large piece of stone fell from the roof and hit him on the head, killing him immediately. The police reported that nobody was on the roof at the time. From papers found on the body they discovered that the dead man was an Englishman, named Karswell.

Some months later Dunning reminded Harrington that he had never told him what his brother had talked about in his sleep. But Harrington had only said a few words when Dunning begged him to stop.

The Experiment

In the last days of December, Dr Hall, the village priest, was working in his study when his servant entered the room, in great alarm.

'Oh, Dr Hall, sir,' she cried. 'What do you think? The poor Squire's dead!'

'What? Squire Bowles? What are you saying, woman?' replied the priest. 'I saw him only yesterday—'

'Yes, sir, I know,' said the servant, 'but it's true. Mr Wickem, the clerk, has just brought the news on his way to ring the church bell. You'll hear it yourself in a moment. Listen! There it is.' And sure enough, the bell then began to ring, long and slow, telling the people of the village that someone had died.

Dr Hall stood up. 'This is terrible,' he said. 'I must go up to the Hall at once. The Squire was so much better yesterday. It seems so sudden.'

'Yes, sir,' agreed the servant. 'Mr Wickem said that the poor Squire was taken ill very suddenly with a terrible pain. He died very quickly, and Wickem said they want him buried quickly too.'

'Yes, yes; well, I must ask Mrs Bowles herself or Mr Joseph,' said the priest. 'Bring me my coat and hat, please.

Oh, and tell Mr Wickem that I would like to see him when he has finished ringing the bell.' And he hurried off to the Hall.

When he returned an hour later, he found the clerk waiting for him.

'There's a lot of work for you to do, Wickem,' he said, 'and not much time to do it.'

'Yes, sir,' said Wickem. 'You'll want the family tomb opened, of course . . .'

'No, no, not at all,' replied Dr Hall. 'The poor Squire said before he died that he did not want to be buried in the family tomb. It is to be an earth grave in the churchyard.'

'Excuse me, sir,' said Wickem, very surprised. 'Do I understand you right? No tomb, you say, and just an earth grave? The poor Squire was too ill to know what he was saying, surely?'

'Yes, Wickem, it seems strange to me too,' said the priest. 'But Mr Joseph tells me that his father, or I should say his stepfather, made his wishes very clear when he was in good health. Clean earth and open air. You know, of course, the Squire had some strange ideas, though he never told me of this one. And there's another thing, Wickem. No coffin.'

'Oh dear, oh dear!' said Wickem. 'There'll be some talk about that. And I know that old Mr Wright has some lovely wood for the Squire's coffin – he's kept it for him for years.'

'Well,' said Dr Hall, 'those are the Squire's wishes, so I'm told, so that's what we must do. You must get the grave dug and everything ready by ten o'clock tomorrow night. Tell Wright that we shall need some lights.'

'Very well, sir. If those are the orders, I must do my best,' said Wickem. 'Shall I send the women from the village to prepare the body?'

'No, Wickem. That was not mentioned,' said the priest. 'No doubt Mr Joseph will send for them if he wants them. You have enough work to do without that. Good night, Wickem.' He paused. 'I was just writing out the year's burials in the church records. I didn't think that I'd have to add Squire Bowles' name to them.'

The Squire's burial took place as planned. All the villagers and a few neighbours were present, and the Squire's stepson Joseph walked behind the body as it was carried to the churchyard. In those days nobody expected the Squire's wife to come to the burial. The Squire had no family except his wife and stepson, and he had left everything to his wife.

But what was everything? The land, house, furniture, pictures, and silver were all there, but no money was found. This was very strange. Squire Bowles was quite a rich man; he received plenty of money from his land every year, his lawyers were honest, but still there was no money. The Squire had not been mean with his money. His wife had all she needed, he sent Joseph to school and university, and he lived well. But still he earnt more money than he spent. Where was it?

Mrs Bowles and her son searched the house and grounds several times but found no money. They could not understand it. They sat one evening in the library discussing the problem for the twentieth time.

'You've been through his papers again, Joseph, have you?' asked the mother.

'Yes, Mother, and I've found nothing.'

'What was he writing the day before he died, do you know? And why was he always writing to Mr Fowler in Gloucester?'

'You know he had some strange ideas about what happens to a person's soul when he dies. He was writing to Mr Fowler

'You've been through his papers again, Joseph, have you?'

about it but he didn't finish the letter. Here, I'll read it to you.'

He fetched some papers from the Squire's writing table and began to read.

My dear friend,

You will be interested to hear about my latest studies, though I am not sure how accurate they are. One writer says that for a time after death a man's soul stays close to the places he knew during life – so close, in fact, that he can be called to speak to the living. Indeed, he must come, if he is called with the right words. And these words are given in an experiment in Dr Moore's book, which I have copied out for you. But when the soul has come, and has opened its mouth to speak, the caller may see and hear more than he wishes, which is usually to know where the dead man has hidden his money.

Joseph stopped reading and there was silence for a moment. Then his mother said, 'There was no more than that?'

'No, Mother, nothing.'

'And have you met this Mr Fowler?'

'Yes. He came to speak once or twice at Oxford.'

'Well,' said the mother, 'as he was a friend of the Squire, I think you should write to him and tell him what . . . what has happened. You will know what to say. And the letter is for him, after all.'

'You're right, Mother,' replied Joseph. 'I'll write to him at once.' And he wrote that same evening.

In time a letter came back from Gloucester and with it a large packet; and there were more evening talks in the library at the Hall. At the end of one evening, the mother said:

'Well, if you are sure, do it tonight. Go round by the fields where no one will see you. Oh, and here's a cloth you can use.'

'What cloth is it, Mother?' asked Joseph.

'Just a cloth,' was the answer.

Joseph went out by the garden door, and his mother stood in the doorway, thinking, with her hand over her mouth. Then she said quietly, 'It was the cloth to cover his face. Oh, I wish I had not been so hurried!'

The night was very dark and a strong wind blew loud over the black fields; loud enough to drown all sounds of calling or answering – if anyone did call or answer.

Next morning Joseph's mother hurried to his bedroom. 'Give me the cloth,' she said. 'The servants must not find it. And tell me, tell me, quick!'

Her son, sitting on the edge of the bed with his head in his hands, looked up at her with wild, red eyes.

'We have opened his mouth,' he said. 'Why, oh why, Mother, did you leave his face uncovered?'

'You know how hurried I was that day,' she replied. 'I had no time. But do you mean that you have seen it?'

Joseph hid his face in his hands. 'Yes, Mother, and he said you would see it, too.'

His mother gave an awful cry and caught hold of the bedpost.

49

'He's angry,' Joseph went on. 'He was waiting for me to call him, I'm sure. I had only just finished saying the words when I heard him – like a dog growling under the earth.'

He jumped to his feet and walked up and down the room.

*'I had only just finished saying the words when I heard him –
like a dog growling under the earth.'*

'And now he's free! What can we do? I cannot meet him again. I cannot take the drink he drank and go where he is! And I'm afraid to lie here another night! Oh, why did you do it, Mother? We had enough as it was.'

'Be quiet!' said his mother through dry lips. 'It was you as much as I. But why spend time talking? Listen to me. It's only six o'clock. Yarmouth's not far, and we've enough money to cross the sea – things like him can't follow us over water. We'll take the night boat to Holland. You see to the horses while I pack our bags.'

Joseph stared at her. 'What will people say here?'

'You must tell the priest that we've learnt of some of the Squire's money in Amsterdam and we must go to collect it. Go, go! Or if you're not brave enough to do that, lie here and wait for him again tonight.'

Joseph trembled and left the room.

That evening after dark a boatman entered an inn at Yarmouth, where a man and a woman were waiting, with their bags on the floor beside them.

'Are you ready, sir and madam?' he asked. 'We sail in less than an hour. My other passenger is waiting by the boat. Is this all your luggage?' He picked up the bags.

'Yes, we are travelling light,' said Joseph. 'Did you say you have other passengers for Holland?'

'Just one,' replied the boatman, 'and he seems to travel even lighter than you.'

'Do you know him?' asked Mrs Bowles. She put her hand

on her son's arm, and they both paused in the doorway.

'No,' said the boatman. 'He keeps his face hidden, but I'd know him again by his voice – he's got a strange way of speaking, like a dog growling. But you'll find that he knows you. "Go and fetch them out," he said to me, "and I'll wait for them here." And sure enough, he's coming this way now.'

In those days women who poisoned their husbands were burnt to death. The records for a certain year at Norwich tell of a woman who was punished in this way, and whose son was hanged afterwards. No one had accused them of their crime, but they told the priest of their village what they had done. The name of the village must remain secret, because people say there is money still hidden there.

Dr Moore's book of experiments is now in the University Library at Cambridge, and on page 144 this is written:

This experiment has often proved true – to find out gold hidden in the ground, robbery, murder, or any other thing. Go to the grave of a dead man, call his name three times, and say: 'I call on you to leave the darkness and to come to me this night and tell me truly where the gold lies hidden.' Then take some earth from the dead man's grave and tie it in a clean cloth and sleep with it under your right ear. And wherever you lie or sleep, that night he will come and tell you truly, waking or sleeping.

'Oh, Whistle, and I'll Come to You, My Boy'

'**A**re you going away for the holidays, Professor?' The speaker was sitting next to the Professor at dinner in St James's College.

'Yes, I'm leaving tomorrow,' said Professor Parkins. 'I'm learning to play golf, and I'm going to Burnstow on the east coast for a week or two to improve my game.'

Professor Parkins was a young man who took himself, and everything that he did, very seriously.

'Oh, Parkins,' said another man. 'There are the remains of an old Templar church at Burnstow. Would you have a look at the place? I'd like to know if it's worth going to see.'

'Certainly,' said the Professor. 'I'll make some notes for you if you like.'

'There won't be much left above ground. I think the place is quite near the beach, about half a mile north from the Globe Inn.'

'I'm staying at the Globe, in fact,' said Parkins. He sounded a little annoyed. 'I could only get a room with two beds in it. I plan to do some work there, and I need a large room with a table, but I really don't like the idea of having two beds in the room.'

'Two beds? How terrible for you, Parkins!' said a man

called Rogers. 'I'll come down and use one of them for a few days. I'll be a companion for you.'

Parkins gave a polite little laugh. 'I'm afraid you'd find it rather dull, Rogers. You don't play golf, do you?'

'No. Very boring game,' said Rogers, not at all politely. 'But if you don't want me to come, just say so. The truth, as you always tell us, never hurts.'

Professor Parkins was well known for always being polite and always telling the truth, and Rogers often amused himself by asking questions which Parkins found difficult to answer. Parkins tried to find an answer now that was both polite and truthful.

'Well, Rogers, perhaps it will be a little difficult for me to work if you are there.'

Rogers laughed loudly. 'Well done, Parkins!' he said. 'Don't worry. I'll let you get on with your work in peace, and I can be useful and keep the ghosts away.' Here he smiled at the others round the table, while Parkins' face turned a deep pink. 'Oh, I'm sorry, Parkins,' Rogers added. 'I forgot that you don't like careless talk about ghosts.'

'That is quite true,' said Parkins. His voice got a little louder. 'I cannot accept the idea of ghosts. It is the complete opposite of everything I believe. I hold, as you know, very strong opinions on this matter.'

'Oh yes, we know that,' said Rogers. 'Well, we'll talk about it again at Burnstow perhaps.'

From this conversation it will be clear that Parkins was indeed a very serious young man – quite unable, sadly, to see the funny side of anything, but at the same time very brave and sincere in his opinions.

Late the following day Parkins arrived at the Globe Inn in Burnstow, and was taken to his room with the two beds, of which we have heard. He unpacked his things and arranged his books and papers very tidily on the large table by the window. In fact, the table was surrounded on three sides by windows: the large central window looked straight out to sea, the right one looked south over the village of Burnstow, and the left one looked north along the beach and the low cliff behind it. Between the inn and the sea, there was only a piece of rough grass and then the beach. Over the years the sea had slowly come closer; now it was no more than fifty metres away.

Most of the people staying at the Globe were there for the golf. One of them was a Colonel Wilson, an old soldier with a very loud voice, and very strong opinions.

Professor Parkins, who was as brave as he was honest, spent the first day of his holiday playing golf with Colonel Wilson, and trying to 'improve his game'. Perhaps he was not wholly successful in this, because by the end of the afternoon the Colonel's face was a most alarming colour. Even his moustache looked angry, and Parkins decided that it would be safer not to walk back to the inn with him. He thought he would walk along the beach instead, and try to find the remains of the Templar church.

He found them very easily – by falling over some of the

Parkins spent the first day trying to 'improve his game'.

old stones, in fact. When he picked himself up, he saw that
the ground all around him was broken up with shallow holes
and bits of old stone wall covered in grass. The Templars
used to build round churches, Parkins remembered, and even
after hundreds of years there were enough grass-covered
stones left to show the circle of the outer wall. For a time
Parkins walked around, looking and measuring, and making
notes in his notebook.

There was a large stone in the centre of the circle, and

Parkins noticed that the grass had been pulled away from one corner of it. He knelt down and, using his pocket-knife, dug away some more of the grass to see the stone underneath. As he did so, a piece of earth fell inwards, showing that there was a hole under the stone. He tried to light a match to see inside, but the wind was too strong, so he put his hand into the hole and felt around with his knife. The sides, top, and bottom of the hole were smooth and regular, he discovered; it must be a man-made hole in a wall. As he pulled the knife out, he heard the sound of metal on metal – there was something in the hole. He put his hand back in and his fingers found a thin piece of metal. Naturally enough, he pulled it out, and saw that it was a piece of metal pipe about ten centimetres long, also man-made and clearly very old. By this time it was getting too dark to do anything more, so he put the metal pipe in his pocket and started to walk home along the beach.

In the evening half-light the place seemed wild and lonely, and a cold north wind blew at his back. Far ahead of him he could see the lights of the village, but here there was only the long empty beach with its black wooden breakwaters, and the shadowy, whispering sea.

He crossed the stones higher up on the beach and went down to the sand, which was easier to walk on, although he had to climb over the breakwaters every few metres.

When he looked behind him to see how far he had come, he saw that he might have a companion on his walk home. A dark figure, some way back, seemed to be running to catch up with him, but he never seemed to get any closer. It couldn't be anybody he knew, Parkins thought, so he did not wait for him. However, a companion, he began to think, would really be very welcome on that cold, dark beach. He suddenly remembered the stories he had read in his less sensible childhood – stories of strange companions met in lonely places. 'What would I do now,' he wondered, 'if I looked back and saw a black figure with wings and a tail? Would I run, or would I stand and fight? Fortunately, the person behind me doesn't look like that – and he seems to be as far away as when I first saw him. I shall get my dinner before he does, and, oh dear! It's nearly time for dinner now. I must run!'

At dinner the Professor found the Colonel much calmer than he had been in the afternoon. Later, the two men played cards together and, as Parkins played cards much better than he played golf, the Colonel became quite friendly and they arranged to play golf together again the next day.

When Parkins returned to his room, he found the little metal pipe where he had put it on the table. He looked at it carefully and realized that it was a whistle. He tried to blow it but it was full of earth, so he took out his knife and cleared the earth out onto a piece of paper, which he then shook out of the window. As he stood at the open window, he was surprised to see someone standing on the grass in front of the hotel, although it was almost midnight.

He shut the window and took the whistle over to the light to look at it again. He cleaned the dirt off and found that there were letters deeply cut along the side of the whistle.

QUIS EST ISTE QUI VENIT

'Now, that's Latin,' he said to himself. 'I think it means, "Who is this who is coming?" Well, the best way to find out is clearly to whistle for him.'

He put the whistle to his lips and blew, then stopped suddenly, surprised and pleased at the sound he had made. It was a soft sound, but also seemed to travel a long way. And it brought a picture into his mind – a picture of a wide, dark place at night, with a fresh wind blowing, and in the middle a lonely figure . . . But at that moment a real wind made his window shake, and the picture disappeared. The wind was so sudden that it made him look up, just in time to see the white shape of a seabird's wing outside the window.

He was so interested in the sound the whistle had made that he blew it again, this time more loudly. No picture came into his mind, but a sudden and very violent wind blew his window open with a crash. Both candles went out, and the wind seemed to be trying to pull the room to pieces. For twenty seconds Parkins battled to close the window again, but it was like trying to push back a burglar who was fighting to get in. Then the wind suddenly dropped for a moment, and the window banged shut and fastened itself. Parkins lit the candles and looked to see what damage had been done. There was none – not even a broken window. But the noise had woken the Colonel in the room above; Parkins could hear him walking around and talking to himself.

Parkins blew the whistle again, this time more loudly.

The wind continued to blow for a long time, beating against the house and crying like a creature in pain. Lying in bed, listening, Parkins thought that a less sensible person might imagine all kinds of unpleasant things. In fact, after a quarter of an hour, he thought that even sensible people would prefer not to hear this sound.

He noticed that one of his neighbours was finding it difficult to sleep, too. He could quite clearly hear someone not far away, turning over in bed again and again.

Sometimes when we close our eyes and try to sleep, we see pictures that are so unpleasant that we have to open our eyes again to make them disappear. This is what now happened to the Professor. Every time he closed his eyes he saw the same picture. There was a long beach with breakwaters running down to the sea, under a dark sky. He recognized it as the beach he had walked along earlier. Then, in the distance, he saw a man running along the beach, climbing desperately over the breakwaters and looking back over his shoulder all the time. Parkins could not see his face, but he knew that the man was terribly afraid. He was also nearly exhausted. Each breakwater was harder to climb than the last. 'Will he get over this next one?' thought Parkins. 'It seems higher than the others.' Yes; half climbing, half throwing himself, the man got over, and then fell to the ground, unable to get up again.

The picture had not yet shown any cause for the man's fear, but now a distant figure appeared, moving very quickly. It wore a long, flowing garment, and there was something so strange about the way it moved that Parkins was very unwilling to see it any closer. It stopped, lifted its arms, bent down towards the sand, then ran, still bent over, down to the edge of the sea and back again. Now it straightened itself, and moved forward along the beach at a frightening speed. At last it came to the breakwater where the man lay hidden. Again it ran down to the sea and back again, then lifted its arms and ran towards the breakwater.

It was always at this moment that Parkins was not brave

enough to keep his eyes closed any longer. At last he decided to light his candle, get out a book, and read for a while. The noise of the match and the sudden light seemed to alarm something near his bed – a rat, probably – which ran away across the floor. The match immediately went out, but a

Every time Parkins closed his eyes he saw the same picture.

second one burnt better, and Parkins lit the candle and opened his book. When he finally felt sleepy, he forgot, for the first time in his tidy, sensible life, to blow out the candle, and the next morning it was completely burnt down.

He was in his room after breakfast when the servant who cleaned the rooms came in, carrying some blankets.

'Would you like any extra blankets on your bed, sir?' she asked.

'Ah, yes, thank you,' said Parkins. 'I would like one. I think it's getting colder.'

'Which bed shall I put it on, sir?' the girl asked.

'What? Why, the one I slept in last night,' replied Parkins.

'Yes, sir. But we thought you'd slept in both of them, sir. We had to make both of them this morning.'

'Really? How strange!' said Parkins. 'I didn't touch the other bed except to put my suitcase on it when I unpacked. But you thought that someone had actually slept in it?'

'Oh yes, sir. The sheets and blankets were thrown all over the place. I thought you'd had bad dreams, sir.'

'Oh dear,' said Parkins. 'Well, I'm sorry if I made extra work for you. Oh, I'm expecting a friend of mine from Cambridge to come for a few days and sleep in the other bed. That will be all right, I suppose?'

'Oh yes, sir,' said the girl. 'It's no trouble, I'm sure. Thank you, sir.' And she left the room.

That day Parkins tried very hard to improve his game, with some success, and the Colonel became even more friendly, and quite talkative.

'That was an extraordinary wind we had last night,' he said as they were playing. 'In my part of the country they would say that someone had been whistling for it.'

'Do they really believe in that kind of thing where you come from?' asked Parkins.

'They believe in it all over the place,' the Colonel replied. 'And, in my experience, there's usually some truth in what the country people say.'

There was a pause in the conversation while they continued with the game. Then Parkins said, 'I feel I should tell you, Colonel, that I hold very strong opinions on these matters. In fact, I don't believe at all in anything supernatural.'

'What?' cried the Colonel, 'D'you mean to say that you don't believe in ghosts, or anything of that kind?'

'In nothing whatever of that kind,' replied Parkins. 'There is an explanation for everything, you see. In fact,' he went on, 'I blew a whistle myself last night, and the wind seemed to come in answer to my call. But of course—'

The Colonel stopped and looked at him. 'Whistling, were you?' he said. 'What kind of whistle did you use? Your turn to play, sir.'

Parkins hit his ball, and then told the Colonel about finding the old whistle in the Templar church.

'Well, sir, I'd be very careful about using a thing like that,' said the Colonel. 'Who knows what the Templars used it for? Dangerous lot of people, they were.'

He went on to give his opinions on the church, old and modern, and the two men had a very enjoyable argument.

The morning passed so pleasantly that they continued to play golf together in the afternoon, then walked back in the evening light to the Globe.

As they turned the corner of the inn, the Colonel was nearly knocked down by a small boy who ran into him at high speed, and then remained holding on to him and crying. At first the Colonel was rather annoyed, but he soon saw that the boy was so frightened that he could not speak.

'What's the matter? What have you seen? Who has frightened you?' the two men asked together.

'Oh sir! I saw it wave at me out of the window,' cried the boy, 'and I don't like it.'

'What window?' said the Colonel crossly. 'Explain yourself, boy.'

'The front window in the inn, sir, upstairs.'

After several questions they learnt that the boy had been playing with his friends on the grass in front of the inn. When the others had gone home for their tea, he had looked up at the big front window and had seen something waving at him. It was a figure of some kind, in white. The boy couldn't see its face, but it had waved at him. There was something horrible about it, and it wasn't like a human being at all.

'It was someone trying to frighten you,' said the Colonel. 'Next time, like a brave little English boy, you throw a stone at it . . . Well, perhaps not that; but tell the people in the inn about it. Now, here's sixpence for you, and you'd better run along home for your tea.'

The two men went round to the front of the inn and looked

up. There was only one window that fitted the description they had heard.

'That's very strange,' said Parkins. 'I remember that I locked my door when I went out this morning and the key is still in my pocket.'

They went upstairs, found that the door of the room was still locked, unlocked it, and went in.

'Well, everything seems perfectly all right,' said Parkins, looking around.

'Except your bed,' said the Colonel.

'That's not my bed,' said Parkins. 'But it certainly looks *very* untidy.' The sheets and blankets were thrown about all over the bed. Parkins thought for a while. 'Ah,' he said, 'I disarranged it when I was unpacking. Perhaps the girl came in to make the bed, the boy saw her at the window, and then she was called away before she could finish it.'

'Well, ring the bell and ask her,' said the Colonel.

When the girl came, she explained that she had made the bed in the morning and that no one had been in the room since the Professor had left. Mr Simpson, the manager, had the only other key. Mr Simpson then came up and said that he had not been in the room himself, and had not given the key to anyone else. Parkins checked the room carefully; nothing was missing and his books and papers were as he had left them. The girl made the bed again and the two men went down to have their tea.

That evening, Colonel Wilson was unusually quiet and thoughtful during dinner and cards and, as they were going up to their rooms, he said to Parkins:

'You know where I am if you need me during the night.'

'Thank you, Colonel, but I don't expect to call on you,' replied Parkins. 'Oh, I have that whistle I told you about. Would you like to see it?'

The Colonel turned the whistle over in his hands, looking at it carefully.

'What are you going to do with it?' he asked.

'I'll show it to the people at Cambridge when I get back and probably give it to the museum, if it's any good.'

'If it were mine,' said the Colonel, 'I'd throw it into the sea right now. But, of course, you and I don't think the same way about these things. Good night.'

And he went off to his room.

There were no curtains at the windows in the Professor's room. The previous night it had not mattered, but tonight there was a bright moon in a cloudless sky. Parkins was afraid that the moonlight might wake him up in the middle of the night, so he arranged a blanket, held up with a stick and his umbrella, which would stop the moonlight shining on to his bed. Soon he was comfortably in bed where he read a book for a while. Then he blew out his candle and went to sleep.

An hour or so later he was suddenly woken by a loud crash. In a moment he realized that the blanket had fallen down and a bright moon was shining on his bed. Should he get up and put the blanket up again, or could he manage to sleep if he did not? He lay in bed for several minutes trying to decide what to do.

All at once he turned over in bed, eyes wide open, listening hard. There had been a movement in the other bed! Was it a rat? The sound came again, something moving in the blankets and making the bed shake. No rat could make a noise like that, surely!

Suddenly his heart nearly stopped beating as a figure sat

There had been a movement in the other bed!

up in the empty bed. Parkins jumped out of his own bed and ran towards the window to get his stick. As he did so, the thing in the other bed slid to the floor and stood, with arms stretched out, between Parkins and the door.

Parkins stared at the creature in horror. He could not reach the door without touching it as he passed, and the thought of that touch made him feel sick.

Now it began to move, bending low and feeling its way with arms that were hidden in its flowing garment. Parkins realized with horror that it could not see. It turned away from him and, in doing so, touched the bed he had just left. It bent its head low and felt all over the bed in a way that made Parkins tremble with fear.

Realizing that the bed was empty, the creature moved forward into the moonlight which shone in through the window. For the first time Parkins saw it clearly, but the only thing he could remember later was a horrible, a sickeningly horrible, face of *crumpled cloth*. The expression on that face he could not or would not describe, but it certainly drove him nearly mad with fear.

But he had no time to watch it for long. With frightening speed the creature moved around the room, searching and feeling, and a corner of its flowing garment brushed across Parkins' face. He screamed in horror, and at once it jumped at him, driving him towards the window. The next moment Parkins was halfway through the window backwards, screaming again and again at the top of his voice, and the cloth face was pushed close into his own.

In that final second, the Colonel kicked the door open and was just in time to see the frightening sight at the window. When he reached the figures, only one was left. Parkins fell forward into the room in a faint, and before him on the floor lay a crumpled bedsheet.

The Colonel asked no questions, but kept everyone out of the room, helped Parkins back to bed and, with a blanket round his shoulders, spent the rest of the night in the other bed.

The next morning Mr Rogers arrived and, to his surprise, was very warmly welcomed by the Professor. The three men discussed what to do for a long time. The Colonel, who remembered a similar experience in India, supposed that the creature, having no body of its own, had to make one out of the sheet from the bed. At the end of their talk, the Colonel left the hotel carrying between his finger and thumb a small piece of metal, which he threw into the sea as far as a strong arm could send it. Later, he burnt the sheet in the field behind the Globe.

As you can imagine, Professor Parkins' opinions on some matters are now less certain than they used to be. He is also a more nervous person than he was. Even a coat hanging up on a door will alarm him, and the sight of a scarecrow in a field late on a winter afternoon has given him more than one sleepless night.

GLOSSARY

alchemy an old kind of chemistry, often used for witchcraft or
   magic

amateur someone who does something (e.g. painting, acting) as
   a hobby, without receiving money for it

artist a person who paints or draws pictures

bitter feeling angry because someone has been unjust to you

breakwater a wall built out into the sea to stop waves
   damaging the coast

candle a stick of wax which is burned to give light

cart a wooden vehicle pulled by horses

casting throwing or putting

chain metal rings joined together in a long 'rope'

churchyard the ground around a church where dead bodies are
   buried

cloth a piece of any kind of material (e.g. cotton, wool)

coffin a box in which a dead body is buried

colonel an army officer

compartment a 'room' on a train

concert a musical performance before an audience

crawl to move slowly on hands and knees

creature a living being, human or non-human

crumpled bent or pushed together untidily; not smooth

description saying in words what something or someone is like

earth the soft part of the ground, not rock or stone

experiment a test done in order to see what happens

expert someone who knows a lot about something

extinct (of a plant, animal, etc.) that no longer exists

faint *(n)* losing consciousness

forehead the part of the face above the eyes and below the hair

gallows a wooden post on which criminals were killed by hanging

garment something you wear; any piece of clothing

golf a game where players hit small balls into holes in the ground

grave *(n)* a hole in the ground in which a dead body is buried

growl *(v)* to make a low angry sound like a dog

guest a person who is invited to visit or stay in a house

hang to kill someone by holding them above the ground with a rope around the neck

heath open wild land

horrible very frightening or unpleasant, causing horror

improve to become better or to make something better

inn a pub or a small old hotel

lamp a light which burns oil

Latin the language of ancient Rome

lawn grass in a garden, which is cut often to keep it short

leaflet a printed piece of paper which contains information

lean *(v)* to rest part of the body on or against something

librarian somebody who works in a library

link *(n)* something that joins two or more things

mind *(n)* the part of a person that thinks and feels

museum a building with interesting things for people to visit

nervous easily worried or frightened

ordinary normal, usual

passage a narrow way through something, with walls on both sides

poison something which causes illness or death if eaten or drunk

priest an official of a church

professor a university teacher

rat a small animal with sharp teeth and a long tail

record *(n)* a written report of facts and events (e.g. births and deaths)

roll *(v)* to move from side to side

runes a very old alphabet, with a mysterious or magic meaning

runic of or belonging to runes

sand the yellow or white soft ground found on beaches

scarecrow a figure made out of sticks and old clothes, and put in a field to frighten birds

soul the part of a person that is believed to go on living after death

squire an important landowner in earlier times

stepfather your mother's husband but not your natural father

stretch to put your arms out and away from your body

supernatural that cannot be explained by the laws of science

telegram a message sent by electrical means, then written and delivered

Templars an organization of fighting men that started in Jerusalem in 1118 and ended in 1312

tomb a grave built of stone under or above the ground

whistle *(n)* a pipe that you blow through to make a clear high sound

witchcraft the use of supernatural or magic powers, usually evil ones

wolf a wild animal that looks like a large dog

Before Reading

1 **Read the introduction on the first page of the book, and the back cover. Can you match the people with the descriptions?**

Mr Williams / Mr Thomson / Mr Dunning /
Squire Bowles' wife / Professor Parkins

1 _____ tries to get information from a dead person.
2 _____ unlocks a door in an inn and sees an awful secret.
3 _____ makes a noise that wakes a frightening creature.
4 _____ sees something very strange in an old picture.
5 _____ touches something horrible which he cannot see.

2 **What kind of ghosts will you find in these stories? Try to guess by matching the two parts of the descriptions together.**

1 A ghost that lives in an inn . . .
2 A creature called up by a whistle . . .
3 A ghost that appears in a picture . . .
4 A ghost called out of its grave . . .
5 A creature called up by runic writing . . .
6 . . . because it knows where money is hidden.
7 . . . and shakes with cold, even in hot sunshine.
8 . . . that takes the shape of a dog and makes the air hot.
9 . . . and steals a child from a house.
10 . . . that does not speak and has no body of its own.

While Reading

**Read *The Picture*. Are these sentences true (T) or false (F)?
Rewrite the false ones with the correct information.**

1 The picture was of an old country church.
2 The first person to see the figure in the picture was Binks.
3 Garwood saw a figure crawling across the lawn.
4 When Nisbet saw the picture, there was no figure on the
   grass, and the house was in sunlight, with an open door.
5 Nisbet thought the creature was doing something terrible
   inside the house.
6 When the figure came out of the house, it was alone.
7 The picture only changed when no one was watching it.
8 Gawdy was hanged, but came back from the grave to kill
   Sir Arthur.

Read *Rats*. Then answer these questions.

Why

1 . . . did Thomson close the door quickly and quietly?
2 . . . did Thomson go upstairs again before leaving the inn?
3 . . . did Thomson fall down in a faint?
4 . . . were Mr and Mrs Betts worried?
5 . . . was the innkeeper hanged?
6 . . . did the fishermen pull down the gallows?
7 . . . hadn't Mr and Mrs Betts ever seen the ghost?

Read to the bottom of page 39 in *Casting the Runes*. What do you think will happen? Choose one of these ideas.

1 Dunning will return the paper to Karswell, who will die.
2 Both Dunning and Karswell will die in a train accident.
3 Dunning will die on July 23rd, as Karswell planned.

Now read the rest of *Casting the Runes*. Choose the best question-word for these questions, and then answer them.

Why / What / How

1 ... was Karswell unpopular with his neighbours?
2 ... happened at Karswell's Christmas party?
3 ... did John Harrington die?
4 ... did Dunning touch in the dark next to his bed?
5 ... was the link between Dunning and John Harrington?
6 ... did Henry Harrington know about 'casting the runes'?
7 ... was the best way to avoid the danger of the 'runes'?
8 ... didn't Karswell recognize Dunning on the train?
9 ... did Dunning manage to give the paper to Karswell?
10 ... did the ticket collector notice when Karswell went onto the boat?
11 ... did Dunning want to send a telegram to France?

Read *The Experiment*. Who said or wrote these words, and to whom? Who, or what, were they talking about?

1 'It seems so sudden.'
2 'Oh dear, oh dear! There'll be some talk about that.'
3 'Yes, Mother, and I've found nothing.'

4 'Indeed, he must come, if he is called with the right words.'
5 'Well, if you are sure, do it tonight.'
6 '. . . and he said you would see it, too.'
7 '. . . things like him can't follow us over water.'
8 'But you'll find that he knows you.'
9 'Go and fetch them out, and I'll wait for them here.'

Read to the bottom of page 67 in '*Oh, Whistle, and I'll Come to You, My Boy*'. Can you guess how the story will end?

1 Parkins' dead body will be found on the beach, and there will be strange marks in the sand.
2 Parkins will be found dead in his bed the next morning, and the whistle will not be there.
3 A frightening creature will try to kill Parkins, but the Colonel will save him.

Now read the rest of the story, and answer these questions.

1 What kind of person was Professor Parkins?
2 What was strange about the dark figure that was following Parkins along the beach?
3 What did Parkins hear and see when he blew the whistle for the first time?
4 Why did Parkins sleep better after he read his book?
5 Why did the servant think he had slept in both beds?
6 What frightened the little boy?
7 What was the most frightening thing about the creature that Parkins found in his room?
8 How did the experience change Parkins?

After Reading

1 **Perhaps this is what some of the characters in the stories were thinking. Which five characters were they (one from each story), and what happens next in the story?**

1 'I think there's someone running up behind me. Who . . . Aargh! What is that awful creature? And it's coming after me! Must run. Get away from it. Faster, faster . . .'

2 'He thinks he's won, but he's wrong. As soon as the moon goes behind a cloud, I'll be in at the window – and I know exactly where to go. And when I've finished, what use will his land and his money be to him then?'

3 'Things have been quiet enough so far, but I don't think I'll go to bed yet – I want to be ready in case . . . Was that a scream? Yes, and I'm sure it came from the room below. I'd better go and see if he's all right . . .'

4 'Why did he want to go upstairs again? What's he doing? I hope he hasn't . . . Good Lord! What was that noise? Here he comes, down the stairs – and he's as white as a sheet. Oh, you stupid young man!'

5 'Only three passengers tonight. That one waiting by the boat is a bit strange. Why won't he show his face? And his voice – it's more like a dog growling. Still, I'd better fetch the other two from the inn – it's time to go.'

2 **Complete these descriptions of *The Picture* with one word in each gap. Then fill in the names of the first person to see the picture like this, and put the descriptions in the right order.**

away, child, closed, country, crawl, cross, door, edge, figure, front, garment, ground, head, house, lawn, middle, moonlight, nobody, open, rows, shone, windows, wore

1 On the lawn in front of the house, a figure was beginning to _____ towards the house. It _____ a strange black _____ with a white _____ on the back.
(*The first person to see the picture like this was _____.*)

2 The moon still _____ on the house, but the window was _____. The figure in black was walking _____ from the house, towards the _____ of the picture. In its arms it held a _____.
(*The first person to see the picture like this was _____.*)

3 The picture showed a large _____ house with three _____ of windows. There was a _____ in the _____ of the bottom row. In front of the house was a large _____.
(*The first person to see the picture like this was _____.*)

4 The picture showed a country house by _____. There was _____ on the grass, but one of the _____ on the _____ floor, on the left of the door, was _____.
(*The first person to see the picture like this was _____.*)

5 The picture showed a house with a lawn. There was a _____ at the _____ of the picture, in the front. It was the _____ of a person who was looking towards the _____.
(*The first person to see the picture like this was _____.*)

3 These parts of sentences tell the end of the story of *Rats*. Put them into the correct order, and use these linking words to join them into a paragraph of four sentences.

after / although / and / but then / until

1 _____ fell down in a faint at the door of the inn.
2 At first he thought the thing on the bed was a scarecrow,
3 _____ he promised never to talk about the ghost.
4 He shut the door with a bang, ran downstairs
5 _____ Thomson's luggage had been put on the cart,
6 _____ he apologized to the innkeeper and his wife,
7 he went upstairs again to look inside the locked room.
8 they felt that they couldn't accept his apologies
9 _____ he realized that it was in fact a ghost.

4 Imagine that Henry Harrington (in *Casting the Runes*) wrote to Mr Bennett to tell him what happened to Karswell. Complete his letter with one suitable word for each gap.

Dear Gordon,

In my last letter I told _____ about Edward Dunning, and the danger _____ was in from the runic message _____ Karswell had given him. I am _____ to tell you that Dunning is _____ longer in danger, and that Karswell _____ make no more trouble for anyone.

_____ Karswell took the train to Dover, _____ and I were in the same _____. Just before we arrived, Dunning managed _____ give the runic paper back. Karswell _____ up to look out of the _____, and his wallet fell to the _____. Dunning quickly picked it up and _____ the paper inside it. Then he _____ the wallet back to Karswell.

Two _____ later in France, Karswell was killed _____ a stone falling from a church _____. It was July 23rd, exactly three _____ after Karswell had given Dunning the _____. I am quite certain Karswell _____ my poor brother's death, and he _____ now been punished by his own _____.

Yours, Henry

5 **Imagine that Mrs Bowles in *The Experiment* went to see Dr Hall and told him the truth about her husband. Complete their conversation, using as many words as you like.**

DR HALL: Mrs Bowles! I thought you were in Amsterdam.

MRS BOWLES: We never left Yarmouth, sir. Something _____, and I had to _____.

DR HALL: Everything, Mrs Bowles? About what?

MRS BOWLES: About the death of my husband. You see, the truth is that he _____.

DR HALL: Poisoned him? Why on earth did you do that?

MRS BOWLES: It was the money. Joseph and I _____. But after the Squire died, we couldn't _____. So we _____.

DR HALL: What kind of experiment?

MRS BOWLES: It was from Dr Moore's book. Joseph went to the grave and asked _____, but then he _____. And now the Squire's angry ghost _____. Oh, help us, Dr Hall – please help us!

81

6 Perhaps Mr Rogers (in *Oh, Whistle, and I'll Come to You, My Boy*) kept a diary. Complete his diary for the day that he arrived at Burnstow, using these notes to help you.

- arrived yesterday / surprised / Parkins pleased to see me
- terrible experience / some kind of supernatural creature
- whistle / ruins of an old Templar church / blew it
- violent wind / terrible dreams / disarranged bed
- next day / he and Colonel / small boy / horrible figure
- last night / creature in other bed / Parkins very frightened
- out of the window / Colonel heard screams / in time
- creature used sheet / no body / face of crumpled cloth
- Colonel took whistle and sheet / Parkins still very nervous
- shall stay for a while / useful / keep ghosts away!

7 Here are some new titles for the stories. Which titles go with which stories? Which titles do you prefer, and why? Now make up a title of your own for each story.

A Lesson for the Professor	A Picture of Revenge
Appointment with Death	The Gallows Scarecrow
Thief in the Night	Talking to the Dead
Whistling for a Wind	Death by Witchcraft
A Growl from the Grave	Behind A Locked Door

8 Which story did you like best, and which did you find the most frightening? Why? Have you ever seen a ghost or experienced something supernatural? Do you know anyone who has? Do you *believe* in ghosts? Why, or why not?

ABOUT THE AUTHOR

Montague Rhodes James was born in Kent in 1862, and grew up in Suffolk. As a young man he was very interested in the ancient world; he won prizes for writing in Latin, and studied archaeology, history, and Christian art and architecture. He became a respected scholar, and spent most of his life in two great colleges – King's College, Cambridge, and Eton College, a famous boys' school. In 1905 he became Provost (or Head) of King's College, and in 1918 he returned to his old school, Eton, and was the Provost there until his death in 1936.

James wrote and published many books and papers on his studies, but he is best remembered today for his ghost stories. His first collection, *Ghost Stories of an Antiquary*, appeared in 1904, and over the years more volumes came out, including *A Thin Ghost and Others* and *A Warning to the Curious*. The *Collected Ghost Stories*, published in 1931, contains nearly all the stories he wrote. Perhaps his most unusual story was 'The Haunted Dolls' House'. He wrote this for a special collection of two hundred tiny books, which were made for the library of a dolls' house given to Queen Mary of England in 1924.

James only wrote about thirty ghost stories, but many people consider him to be among the best writers in this category. He had three rules for writing ghost stories: there should be no long and complicated information about ghostly practices; the stories should happen in ordinary places and to ordinary people; and, most importantly, the ghost should be evil and eager to hurt or frighten people. Because of his studies, James knew a lot about ancient places, old churches and buildings, and in these calm and peaceful settings he quietly leads his readers to the horror waiting in the shadows. All these things together make his stories very powerful, and many other writers have taken James's ghost stories as a model.

James, known as 'Monty' to his friends, was not just a dry scholar. He was very popular with students, enjoyed the theatre, loved reading detective stories, and his purpose in writing ghost stories was to give 'pleasure of a certain sort'. Many of the stories he read out loud to his friends, while sitting by the fireside at Christmas. He was often asked if he believed in ghosts himself, but he was too clever a scholar to give a clear answer one way or the other. This is what he wrote in the introduction to one of his books: 'Do I believe in ghosts? I am prepared to consider evidence and accept it if it satisfies me.'

ABOUT BOOKWORMS

OXFORD BOOKWORMS LIBRARY
Classics • True Stories • Fantasy & Horror • Human Interest
Crime & Mystery • Thriller & Adventure

The OXFORD BOOKWORMS LIBRARY offers a wide range of original and adapted stories, both classic and modern, which take learners from elementary to advanced level through six carefully graded language stages:

Stage 1 (400 headwords)	**Stage 4** (1400 headwords)
Stage 2 (700 headwords)	**Stage 5** (1800 headwords)
Stage 3 (1000 headwords)	**Stage 6** (2500 headwords)

More than fifty titles are also available on cassette, and there are many titles at Stages 1 to 4 which are specially recommended for younger learners. In addition to the introductions and activities in each Bookworm, resource material includes photocopiable test worksheets and Teacher's Handbooks, which contain advice on running a class library and using cassettes, and the answers for the activities in the books.

Several other series are linked to the OXFORD BOOKWORMS LIBRARY. They range from highly illustrated readers for young learners, to playscripts, non-fiction readers, and unsimplified texts for advanced learners.

Oxford Bookworms Starters   *Oxford Bookworms Factfiles*
Oxford Bookworms Playscripts   *Oxford Bookworms Collection*

Details of these series and a full list of all titles in the OXFORD BOOKWORMS LIBRARY can be found in the *Oxford English* catalogues. A selection of titles from the OXFORD BOOKWORMS LIBRARY can be found on the next pages.

BOOKWORMS · FANTASY & HORROR · STAGE 4
Dr Jekyll and Mr Hyde
ROBERT LOUIS STEVENSON

Retold by Rosemary Border

You are walking through the streets of London. It is getting dark and you want to get home quickly. You enter a narrow side-street. Everything is quiet, but as you pass the door of a large, windowless building, you hear a key turning in the lock. A man comes out and looks at you. You have never seen him before, but you realize immediately that he hates you. You are shocked to discover, also, that you hate him.

Who is this man that everybody hates? And why is he coming out of the laboratory of the very respectable Dr Jekyll?

BOOKWORMS · CRIME & MYSTERY · STAGE 4
Death of an Englishman
MAGDALEN NABB

Retold by Diane Mowat

It was a very inconvenient time for murder. Florence was full of Christmas shoppers and half the police force was already on holiday.

At first it seemed quite an ordinary murder. Of course, there are always a few mysteries. In this case, the dead man had been in the habit of moving his furniture at three o'clock in the morning. Naturally, the police wanted to know why. The case became more complicated. But all the time, the answer was right under their noses. They just couldn't see it. It was, after all, a very ordinary murder.

The Hound of the Baskervilles

SIR ARTHUR CONAN DOYLE

Retold by Patrick Nobes

Dartmoor. A wild, wet place in the south-west of England. A place where it is easy to get lost, and to fall into the soft green earth which can pull the strongest man down to his death.

A man is running for his life. Behind him comes an enormous dog – a dog from his worst dreams, a dog from hell. Between him and a terrible death stands only one person – the greatest detective of all time, Sherlock Holmes.

The Songs of Distant Earth and Other Stories

ARTHUR C. CLARKE

Retold by Jennifer Bassett

'High above them, Lora and Clyde heard a sound their world had not heard for centuries – the thin scream of a starship coming in from outer space, leaving a long white tail like smoke across the clear blue sky. They looked at each other in wonder. After three hundred years of silence, Earth had reached out once more to touch Thalassa . . .'

And with the starship comes knowledge, and love, and pain.

In these five science-fiction stories Arthur C. Clarke takes us travelling through the universe into the unknown but always possible future.

The Whispering Knights

PENELOPE LIVELY

Retold by Clare West

'I don't know that you have done anything wrong,' Miss Hepplewhite said. 'But it is possible that you have done something rather dangerous.'

William and Susie thought they were just playing a game when they cooked a witch's brew in the old barn and said a spell over it, but Martha was not so sure. And indeed, the three friends soon learn that they have called up something dark and evil out of the distant past . . .

Ghost Stories

RETOLD BY ROSEMARY BORDER

After dinner we turned the lights out and played 'hide-and-seek'. In the dark, I touched a hand, a very cold hand. Now, because of the game, I had to hide in the dark with . . . with this cold person – not speaking, not knowing who it was. Slowly the others found us, hid with us, until we were all there – all thirteen. Thirteen? But there were only twelve people in the house! We touched each other in the dark, counting. Thirteen. Quickly, nervously, I lit a match to see . . .